KU-519-230

The Story of
JOSEPH
AND HIS
BROTHERS

Retold by Susan Dickinson
Illustrated by Sally Holmes

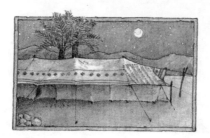

CARNIVAL

In Joseph's family there were twelve boys. Joseph was the favourite, and his father, Jacob, loved him dearly.

Jacob liked to give Joseph special
presents. One day, he gave him a
coat, made of many pieces of
different coloured cloth.

Joseph loved his many-coloured coat, but his brothers were very jealous and refused to talk to him. So Joseph was left to look after his flocks by himself.

One night, Joseph had a strange dream. He dreamed that he and his brothers were binding sheaves of corn in the field. One of his sheaves stood up and his brothers' sheaves stood up in a circle round it, and bowed to it.

When Joseph told the dream to his brothers they were disgusted.
"Don't imagine we're going to bow down to you!" they said.

A few weeks later Joseph had
another strange dream. This time he
dreamed that the sun and moon and
eleven stars all bowed to him.

After this dream his brothers would
have nothing to do with him at all
and led their flocks away to far-off
pastures.

But after they had been gone for
some weeks their father was worried
about them and sent Joseph to look
for them, to bring back news that
they were safe.

When Joseph's brothers saw him coming, they said: "Now's our chance. Let's kill him and throw his body into this dried-up well." But the eldest brother said, "No, don't let's kill him. Let's just throw him in, and leave him."

The others agreed, and when Joseph
came up to them, they knocked him
down, tore off his beautiful coat and
threw him in the well.

Joseph lay at the bottom, bruised and hurt, and wondered how he would ever get out. After a while he heard the sound of camels and many voices. Then he heard his brothers bargaining with the camel drivers. They were planning to sell him!

A rope was let down into the well
and Joseph was hauled out. The
camel drivers gave Joseph's brothers
20 pieces of silver. And they
continued their journey, with
Joseph, to Egypt.

When Joseph had gone, his brothers
killed a goat and dipped Joseph's
many-coloured coat into its blood.
Then they started for home,
carrying Joseph's blood-stained
coat.

Jacob had been waiting anxiously for news of the boys, and when he saw them returning, without Joseph, he ran to meet them. They showed him the blood-stained coat and told him they had found it. Jacob recognized it immediately, and he felt certain that Joseph must be dead.

Joseph's father was very sad and he
wept for his favourite son. But there
was no need for tears, for Joseph
was safe. When the camel drivers
reached Egypt they sold him to the
Captain of the Palace Guard – a
kind man called Potiphar.

Joseph lived happily in Potiphar's
house. He was a hard worker and
soon Potiphar put him in charge of
the running of the whole household.

Carnival
An imprint of the Children's Division
of the Collins Publishing Group
8 Grafton Street, London W1X 3LA

Published by Carnival 1988

Text © 1986 William Collins Sons & Co. Ltd.
Illustrations © 1986 Sally Holmes

ISBN 0 00 194464 9

Printed & bound in Great Britain by
PURNELL BOOK PRODUCTION LIMITED
A MEMBER OF BPCC plc
All rights reserved.